Steam Around
Devon and
Cornwall

Peter W. Gray

Ian Allan
PUBLISHING

Right: There were days when railway staff struggled
to keep the wheels turning, and this was one of
them. Screwing up their eyes against the northerly
blizzard sweeping across Lydford station, the crew
of 2-6-2T No 5564 exchange a few words with the
stationmaster before setting off for Tavistock with
the 12.40pm from Launceston on the branch's 'Last
Day', 29 December 1962.

All photographs by the author

Introduction

Welcome to another celebration of steam in the South West peninsula, as seen through my camera lens during the latter years of regular steam operation. In presenting this further volume, which contains many branch as well as main-line scenes, I have consciously tried to present fresh views, repeating as few as possible of the locations featured in my previous books.

Our journey commences close to Burlescombe, near the Devon/Somerset border, and proceeds at first in a generally westward direction, with diversions to cover most of the branch lines in Devon and Cornwall. We visit the Culm Valley, Tiverton and Exe Valley lines before making an excursion into East Devon, including Lyme Regis, and Exmouth trains.

In those days local passengers had the alternative of the coastal route from Exeter to Newton Abbot or the very rural Teign Valley line, with connection at Heathfield onto the Moretonhampstead branch. We cover both, before journeying down the Kingswear branch to its nerve centre at Paignton.

From high summer at Goodrington beach, we move to Christmas frost at Newton Abbot, before scaling the heights of Dainton Bank, and taking a trip beside the cool waters of the River Dart to Ashburton. Beyond Totnes, there is Rattery Bank to ascend before diverting at Brent to visit the Kingsbridge branch and from Plymouth taking a frosty trip to Launceston.

A reminder of the Southern's erstwhile local services to Plymstock and Turnchapel is followed by views on the Callington line and Southern main line near Brentor. The scene now moves east to Coleford Junction, where the Southern's Plymouth and Ilfracombe lines part company, for a journey towards Ilfracombe, before returning to Torrington, and then hopping across country to Okehampton, whence the so-called 'Withered Arm' can be savoured, concluding with a Beattie well tank venturing out to Wenford Bridge.

The run home commences from Penzance, via St Ives, Hayle and Helston, to St Agnes and Truro. The clay line to Drinnick Mill is not forgotten, nor the 'main' Newquay branch from Par. Much of the charm of Cornwall lay in its short branch lines along river banks to the sea shore, so the Fowey and Looe lines are both visited, along with the overland route to Wadebridge from Bodmin Road.

We leave Cornwall over the Royal Albert Bridge, appropriately in one of the 'sandwich' auto trains which serviced Saltash before the road bridge brought eternal traffic jams, and continue 'over the banks' to terminate our journey at Newton Abbot, where we run out of pages!

I'm sometimes asked how I used to get about while taking these pictures, and, while some were taken while travelling by train, the majority came from the saddle of my water-cooled 200cc LE Velocette motor-cycle. While this was not fast, it was fast enough for the roads and lanes of those days, and utterly reliable. This was, of course, well before helmets became compulsory, and I have fond memories, from the very hot summer of 1959, of setting off from Torquay for Cornwall in the early hours, clad only in shirt and trousers, with the cameras in a haversack, knowing it was going to be hot and sunny all day. And it was.

One advantage of taking a motor-cycle to Cornwall early on summer Saturday mornings, was knowing that you could always get on the first Torpoint ferry, whereas before the road bridge cars could spend two or three hours in the ferry queue on the Plymouth side, waiting to cross the River Tamar.

First published 2001

ISBN 0 7110 2834 6

Published by Ian Allan Publishing

an imprint of Ian Allan Publishing Ltd, Hersham, Surrey KT12 4RG.

Printed by Ian Allan Printing Ltd,
Hersham, Surrey KT12 4RG.

Code: 0110/B2

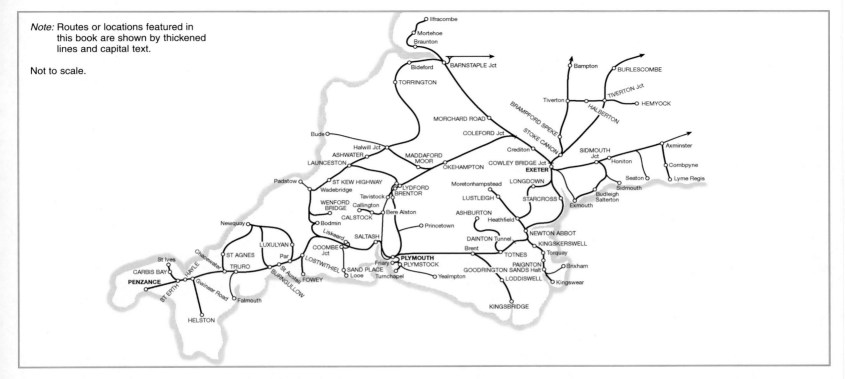

Note: Routes or locations featured in this book are shown by thickened lines and capital text.

Not to scale.

Reproduction is from original slides, mainly Kodachrome I, with Kodachrome II taking over from 1962, and a couple each of High Speed Ektachrome and Agfa CT18. The latter were only used in order to keep going during the winter months, because at a speed of 8 on the Weston meter, Kodachrome I was almost impossible to use other than in good light.

The cameras used were a Voigtlander Vito IIa with a f3.5 Color-Skopar lens, until early 1959, and then an Agfa Super Silette with a f2 Solagon lens and that was in turn replaced by a Pentax S1a during 1965. The first two were both fixed-lens cameras and the fastest shutter speed I could use on Kodachrome I with the Vito IIa was 1/125th sec. The f2 Solagon was a tremendous advance, giving good depth of field and crisp definition to the edges, even at f2. Without it, many of these pictures could not have been taken.

In passing, we must not forget the legion of permanent-way staff who kept the vegetation in check on an annual basis, not on the 30-year basis that seems to be the rule nowadays.

Thanks also to Eric Youldon for the background to the Exeter Central picture, to the publishers for their confidence in asking for another selection of my West Country pictures, and most of all to you, the reader. I hope you will enjoy the selection I have chosen.

Peter W. Gray
Torquay
April 2001

Left: In 1962, when the Spring Bank Holiday was still tied to the religious calendar, the Whitsun Bank Holiday weekend began on the penultimate Saturday of the railway's winter timetable, resulting in a considerably enhanced service. One of the many 'extra' trains was the 10.5am from Paignton to Paddington, which appears to be going well between Burlescombe and Whiteball Siding signalbox behind 4-6-0 No 5067 *St Fagan's Castle* on 9 June 1962.

Above: Later the same day, the crew of 2-8-0 No 2892 seem to be confident they have a clear road ahead as they plod through Tiverton Junction at 4.50pm with an up goods train. In the background, 0-4-2T No 1462 simmers while awaiting its 5.7pm departure to Hemyock.

Above: Alongside the placid waters of the River Culm, 0-4-2T No 1451 pulls out a rake of bulk milk tanks from the sidings behind Hemyock station on 2 December 1961. Meanwhile, the branch passenger coach, an ex-Barry Railway gas-lit vehicle, has been parked on a siding, out of the way.

Right: From arrival at Hemyock at 2.23pm, there were 37 minutes for the shunting to be completed, and water taken, before departure was due at 3.0pm, often with five or six loaded milk tanks ahead of the passenger coach. On the same day, as the December sun sinks to the horizon, 0-4-2T No 1451 leaves the milk factory behind, and the station is almost hidden by steam. The red-brick building on the left was erected by a 19th-century entrepreneur as a refreshment room, but spent most of its life as a farm building.

Above: It is a little ironic that Halberton Halt, opened in 1927, when the GWR publicity machine was in full flow, was constructed in a position which ensured it was almost invisible to people passing along the road above. Were it not for a timetable board announcing 'Halberton Halt' to passers-by, its presence beneath, occupying the space left for a second broad-gauge track never laid, could have gone unnoticed. On 24 March 1962, the 2.22pm from Tiverton Junction, propelled by 0-4-2T No 1471, has stopped beneath the road bridge. Bicycle thieves appear to have been confined to the towns and cities in those days!

Right: In a view typical of the Exe Valley's wooded hills and lush meadows, the 3.20pm from Bampton is propelled south, passing the hamlet of Fairby between Cove and Bolham Halts, by 0-4-2T No 1450 on 16 March 1963.

Left: Originally a full station with stationmaster and signalbox, Brampford Speke, the first station on the Exe Valley line after it left the main line at Stoke Canon, was demoted to Halt status back in 1923. It was unusual in having no road access whatsoever, only a footpath to the village, which is on the far side of the river Exe. Even this footpath floods in periods of heavy rainfall, so it is perhaps surprising that both the station building and the house alongside are still lived in today. 0-4-2T No 1451 pulls away with the 12.48pm from Exeter St David's on 15 June 1963.

Above: 0-4-2T No 1468 drifts into Stoke Canon station with the 9.27am from Dulverton to Exeter St David's on 21 June 1960, only a few days after this station had closed. Paradoxically, Brampford Speke, which the GWR had sought to close when Stoke Canon station was moved to this site in 1894, remained open until October 1963.

Above: Cowley Bridge Junction on 12 March 1960, as 'Battle of Britain' class Pacific No 34063 *229 Squadron* joins the ex-GWR main line from Taunton, with the through Plymouth to Brighton via Okehampton service.

Right: At Exeter Central station, in the gathering gloom of a January afternoon, passengers await departure time, as 'West Country' class 4-6-2 No 34015 *Exmouth* prepares to haul them back to Salisbury on 8 January 1966. This privately sponsored railtour in aid of the Woking Children's Home was one of several 'Last Steam to Exeter' railtours around this time. The Waterloo to Salisbury leg was handled both ways by No 34001 *Exeter*.

Left: With only four coaches on the draw-bar, 'Battle of Britain' class Pacific No 34109 *Sir Trafford Leigh-Mallory* sprints up the 1-in-80 incline to Honiton tunnel with the 3.5pm Salisbury to Exeter stopper on 18 June 1960.

Above: The Lyme Regis branch had been built under the 'Light Railway' regulations, which allowed curves more severe than those encountered on a normal branch line, and it was the tight curves which enabled these elegant 4-4-2Ts of the London & South Western Railway's '415' class to continue in service until 1961, despite several attempts to replace them. This engine was built as LSWR No 488 by Neilson & Co in 1885 and was sold out of service by the LSWR in 1917 to the Ministry of Munitions, which in turn later sold it to the East Kent Railway, from where it was bought back by the Southern Railway in 1946 and put to work on the branch, along with the other two survivors. No 30583 is climbing to Combpyne with the 12.40pm from Axminster on 18 June 1960.

Above: This view of Sidmouth Junction station, taken from the end of the goods shed line at 3.54pm on 15 August 1964, shows a rebuilt 'West Country' class Pacific, possibly No 34013 *Okehampton*, on a non-stop down train, probably a military special. Through the arch of the goods shed can be seen BR Standard Class 3 2-6-2T No 82042, which will head the 4.0pm stopper to Exeter Central, while the new diesel multiple-unit is working the 4.5pm service to Exmouth.

Right: One of several summer Saturday trains from east Devon to Waterloo via Sidmouth Junction on 10 August 1963, the 9.30am from Exmouth surmounts the ridge before dropping down into Budleigh Salterton, behind BR Standard Class 4 2-6-4Ts Nos 80035 and 80064. Across the bay, Teignmouth appears to be enjoying a burst of sunlight.

Left: Wolverhampton appears to have 'borrowed' a Shrewsbury engine, 4-6-0 No 6956 *Mottram Hall*, to work the 10.18am to Paignton on Saturday 6 August 1960. While rounding the curves at Powderham, the passengers' attention will be torn between the views of the River Exe estuary on one side, and the Earl of Devon's deer, grazing in the grounds of Powderham Castle, on the landward side.

Above: Close to high tide on the River Exe, 4-6-0 No 6025 *King Henry III* steams through Starcross with the 8.0am from Kingswear to Paddington on 29 July 1961. In the background can be seen Starcross signalbox and the truncated tower of Brunel's Atmospheric Pump House. This view was taken from the steps of a navigation light that no longer exists — only the pier on which it once stood remains.

PASSENGERS
ARE NOT ALLOWED TO
CROSS THE RAILWAY
EXCEPT BY THE BRIDGE

Left: 4-6-0 No 5913 *Rushton Hall* pulls slowly into Newton Abbot at 7.22am on 29 July 1961, probably after a tedious run down from Exeter, stopping in each section from Exminster to Newton Abbot East, the signalbox visible above the last four coaches. The train is one of the many reliefs and duplicates which ran on that Friday night/Saturday morning, probably originating in the Sheffield/Leeds/Bradford area. Tucker's Maltings still trades from the buildings on the left, which date back to the 1870s.

Above: Longdown station was at the summit of the Teign Valley line, situated in a well-wooded area of the Haldon Hills, between two tunnels — Culver Tunnel on the Christow side and Perridge Tunnel towards Exeter. With passenger bookings as low as one per day in winter, the signalman on duty here had a lonely life. Although the loop was removed in 1954, Longdown remained a block post until the line closed in June 1958. On 22 June 1957 venerable auto trailers Nos W93W and W98W form the 1.5pm from Heathfield, now departing for its timetable destination at Exeter St Thomas behind 2-6-2T No 5536. Both auto trailers were withdrawn later that year.

Above: Not looking at its best during the final few months of the passenger service, Lustleigh had for many years, both before and after World War 2, won Garden Certificates in the GWR's annual station competition. On 27 December 1958, 0-4-2T No 1466 pauses with the 12.50 service from Newton Abbot to Moretonhampstead while a few passengers alight. Coal is still being delivered to the Lustleigh merchant, but the Camping Coach which occupied the station end of this siding each summer until 1958 has returned to Swindon from its final visit to Lustleigh. Lustleigh villagers remained loyal to the railway to the end, and outnumbered travellers from any of the other stations in the branch's last few years.

Right: At the Newton Abbot end of the Moretonhampstead branch, 2-6-2T No 5153 waits while the crossing gates are opened at Teignbridge Crossing on 11 June 1962. The 'South Devon Phoenix' had been organised by the South Devon Railway Society, which at that time still hoped to preserve the line to Moretonhampstead. Alongside the train is a loading platform used by the ball clay industry for exporting its product, in earlier days to Teignmouth docks but latterly mainly to Staffordshire.

Left: On summer Saturdays the Torbay road crossing in the centre of Paignton tended to govern the passage of trains along the Kingswear branch, because the throng of pedestrians and traffic was such that the signalman in Paignton North signalbox sometimes had great difficulty in opening the gates. However, on this day, 5 August 1961, it was the late arrival of overnight trains from the north which was delaying the departure of some up morning trains from Paignton. Trains were taking so long to get from Newton Abbot to Paignton that the up trains were due to leave before their engines had arrived! 4-6-0 No 4967 *Shirenewton Hall* has not suffered directly in this way, because it is working the 10.20am Kingswear to Manchester and had an adequate turn round time at the terminus, but it had been held outside Paignton for some time before being allowed in, and did not arrive until 11.26am, with a scheduled departure at 10.44am.

Above: 4-6-0 No 6021 *King Richard II* departs Paignton, over the Torbay road crossing, with the 4.25pm relief to Paddington on 7 June 1960. Above the tender can be seen the old Paignton Picture House, and beyond the shops with their decorative top floors can be glimpsed the domed roof of Dellers Café, a much-loved local rendezvous, sadly demolished a few years later.

Above: During the 1950s the sight of an ex-GWR freight 2-8-0 heading a summer Saturday relief was not exceptional, but by 1961 the BR Standard '9F' class 2-10-0s had taken over this role. Thus it was with some surprise, as I stood on Kingskerswell station's up platform at 3.5pm on 5 August 1961, that I found 2-8-0 No 3854 approaching with train No 1C66 bound for Paignton.

Right: With Goodrington south sands packed on a gloriously hot Sunday afternoon, 4-6-0 No 7003 *Elmley Castle* struggles to lift the augmented 2.20pm Exeter St David's to Kingswear stopper away from Goodrington Sands Halt on 5 July 1959.

Left: In the opposite conditions to those on the previous page, Bristol Bath Road 'Modified Hall' class 4-6-0 No 7901 *Dodington Hall* waits in Newton Abbot's No 4 platform, while Christmas parcels are unloaded at 9.00am on 22 December 1962.

Above: As 4-6-0 No 6016 *King Edward V* emerges from Dainton Tunnel and races down the bank with the up 'Royal Duchy', 2-8-0 No 3841, assisted by 2-6-2T No 5154 at the rear, heads a Class H freight westwards at 2.50pm on 11 March 1960.

Above: Across the River Dart from the grounds of Dartington Hall, 0-4-2T No 1470 hurries towards Totnes with the 4.10pm service from Ashburton on 3 May 1958. An example of the compromise which had to be made between shutter speed and depth of field when using the extremely slow Kodachrome I film.

Right: In the early days of preservation on the Ashburton branch, on the day the weedkilling train had paid its first visit for several years, 0-4-2T No 1420 shunts at the terminus at Ashburton on 14 May 1966, three years before the Buckfastleigh end of the line re-opened to the public.

Left: On Sundays during the summer of 1959 the down 'Cornish Riviera Express' was still a regular 'King' working, normally piloted from Newton Abbot to Plymouth by a 'Manor'. On the lower slopes of Rattery Bank, just outside Totnes, 4-6-0s No 7818 *Granville Manor* and No 6021 *King Richard II* grapple with the full 14-coach 'chocolate and cream' formation on 9 August 1959.

Above: With Kingsbridge signalbox only just visible behind the train on the far left, 2-6-2T No 5573 pulls away from the terminus, amid a mixture of steel and wooden post signals, with the 12.20pm 'mixed' to Brent on 3 June 1961.

Above: After leaving Kingsbridge, up trains had a short climb to Sorley Tunnel before plunging down into the Avon Valley and then following the river for most of the way to Brent. Loddiswell station, across the river from the village, lay at the foot of the drop into the valley; 2-6-2T No 4561 pulls away with the 11am from Kingsbridge on 16 April 1960. The two Camping Coaches are probably waiting for their first residents of the season.

Right: The approach to Plymouth, between Tavistock Junction and Laira, has suffered drastic change since this picture was taken on 29 April 1961 of 0-6-0PT No 4679 running in towards Laira on the down goods line. Sadly, a six-lane dual carriageway now occupies the area on the left, which was then Blagdon's boatyard, behind which ran the track of the Plymouth & Dartmoor Railway, later the Lee Moor Tramway.

Above: As is usual in South Devon, the morning sun is quickly melting the overnight frost as 2-6-2T No 5569 prepares to leave Plymouth with the 10.40am departure to Launceston on the penultimate Saturday of the passenger service on this line, 22 December 1962.

Right: At Launceston at 12.15pm the same day, the frost is still in evidence, as 2-6-2T No 4591, its hand-painted buffer-beam number unfortunately hidden by a buffer, shunts the branch goods outside the ex-GWR engine shed, which was still in use at that time.

Left: Between Lydford and Tavistock the LSWR's line into Plymouth was built alongside the GWR's earlier Launceston branch. Both lines passed close to Brentor, in the left background, but only the LSWR provided a station for North Brentor village, the GWR preferring to serve the larger Mary Tavy village, nearer to Tavistock. A lucky splash of sunlight falls upon 2-6-2T No 5569 on the 2.5pm from Launceston to Plymouth on 4 August 1962.

Above: On the eastern side of Plymouth the LSWR operated trains from Friary station out to Turnchapel via Plymstock. Under British Railways the passenger service to Turnchapel closed in 1951, but it was re-created on 2 May 1959 for the benefit of passengers on the Railway Correspondence & Travel Society's Plymouth District Tour. Yeovil's ex-LSWR 'O2' class 0-4-4T No 30182 is seen at Plymstock station with the 'gated' set, awaiting the arrival of its passengers.

Above: One of the last regular beats for the ex-LSWR 'O2' class 0-4-4Ts in passenger service in the West Country was on the Callington branch. After leaving the main line at Bere Alston and crossing the River Tamar into Cornwall on Calstock Viaduct, this line then climbed circuitously around Calstock church to come abreast of the old incline that took the earlier East Cornwall Mineral Railway wagons down to the riverside quays. As No 30225 climbs towards Gunnislake on 15 April 1961, the head of the old incline is only about a quarter of a mile to the right.

Right: The same train is seen again beyond Chilsworthy Halt, the stop after Gunnislake. The halt is alongside the background road bridge, amid the relics of this valley's industrial past. Mine chimneys and engine houses abound, and abandoned mineshafts are an ever-present hazard in the area. By the 1960s, apart from quarrying, the industrial activity was all horticultural, in this area favoured for its early season's produce.

Left: The first of two more pictures taken in the Brentor area. This view is between Lydford and Brentor and features the 11.0am Exeter Riverside Yard to Plymouth Western Region goods, running under Class H, behind Exeter's 2-6-0 No 7311 on 15 April 1961. Probably run only to retain Western Region drivers' route knowledge of the Okehampton line, the similar Southern freight over the GWR's coastal route had been dropped at (or very soon after) the end of the war.

Above: This time the sun is on Brentor as well, as 'Battle of Britain' class Pacific No 34080 *74 Squadron* rolls down the valley towards Tavistock with the 9.3am from Portsmouth to Plymouth on 4 August 1962.

Two views taken near Coleford Junction, where the North Devon line parts company with the Southern's 'main line' to Plymouth, both taken on 20 June 1964.

Left: Running up, but mainly downhill, from Okehampton towards the junction comes 'N' class 2-6-0 No 31840 with the combined 8.30am from Padstow and 9.30am from Bude, bound for Waterloo.

Above: Later that afternoon the same engine returns, now hauling the 10.35am from Waterloo to Bude (arr 3.55pm) and Padstow (arr 5.0pm) portions of the down 'Atlantic Coast Express'. This time we can see the broad sweeping curve of the North Devon line as it climbs to Copplestone.

Left: Although the North Devon line was double-track to Copplestone, beyond here it became single as far as Umberleigh, with (until 1964) passing loops at each station. The first station on the single-track section was Morchard Road, situated some two miles from Morchard Bishop, and the least-used station on the line. On 5 August 1963 'Battle of Britain' class 4-6-2 No 34065 *Hurricane* runs in with the rear portion of the 9.0am from Waterloo, stopping at each station from Exeter Central to Barnstaple Junction.

Above: At Barnstaple Junction station on 26 August 1963, 2-6-0 No 7326 stands at the head of the 10.50am to Taunton. The skeleton of the engine shed houses 'N' class 2-6-0 No 31849, and 'West Country' Pacific No 34020 *Seaton*, while taking water outside is Ivatt Class 2 2-6-2T No 41224.

Left: Between Barnstaple Junction and Braunton the Ilfracombe branch was almost level, but beyond Braunton the gradient steepened, culminating in a 3½-mile climb at 1 in 40 to Mortehoe & Woolacombe station. On summer Saturdays several of the Taunton to Barnstaple Junction trains were extended to Ilfracombe; on 27 July 1963 2-6-0 No 6346 starts the 1-in-40 climb near Pines Dean, assisted at the rear by Ivatt Class 2 2-6-2T No 41298, with the 8.50am departure from Taunton.

Above: Later that same evening, approaching Heddon Mill Crossing, ex-SR 'N' class 2-6-0 No 31856 and ex-GWR 2-6-0 No 6327 are sailing down the 1 in 40 with the 6.37pm from Ilfracombe to Taunton, having earlier climbed the 1 in 36 out of Ilfracombe.

Run by a joint committee of the Railway Correspondence & Travel Society and the Plymouth Railway Circle, the 'Exmoor Ranger' enjoyed a perfect spring day for the trip from Exeter to North Devon and Somerset on 27 March 1965.

Left: From the slopes of the hill leading up to Great Torrington, we look down on the train as it emerges from the wooded valley which stretches back to Watergate Halt. Headed by Ivatt Class 2 2-6-2Ts Nos 41206 and 41291, the train slows for acceptance into Torrington station, across the River Torridge.

Above: The train now has the road into the station and is crossing the river by the 'new' railway bridge. Alongside can be seen the piers of the original timber viaduct which carried the former 3ft-gauge Marland Light Railway trains. Corresponding 'old' and 'new' road bridges are visible in the background.

Above: At Okehampton on 4 August 1964, BR Standard Class 4 2-6-4T No 80042 prepares to leave with the 1.30pm service to Bude, as Ivatt Class 2 2-6-2T No 41317 and 'N' class 2-6-0 No 31406 pull out of the military sidings with a short ballast train.

Right: With a backdrop of the high tors of Dartmoor, 'West Country' class 4-6-2 No 34107 *Blandford Forum* leads the Padstow and Bude portions of the down 'Atlantic Coast Express' from Meldon Junction towards Maddaford Moor Halt on 4 August 1964.

Left: Even on summer Saturdays, there were only six trains each way that stopped at Ashwater, and roughly the same on weekdays. There was thus plenty of time for a spot of gardening between trains, and on 22 August 1964 the lady of the house appeared to be taking due advantage of this before getting the lunch.

Above: Another seldom-photographed station on the so-called 'Withered Arm' was St Kew Highway. The preserved 'T9' class 4-4-0 No 120, then in LSWR livery, waits with the 'North Cornishman', an earlier RCTS/PRC railtour, to cross an up train from Padstow on 27 April 1963.

Left: The three ex-LSWR Beattie 2-4-0 well tanks were nearing the end of their 67-year reign on the Wenford Bridge line as No 30585 proceeded towards the end of the line with the daily goods train on 13 July 1961. It appears to have been the practice to leave empty vans for loading on the 'main line' at the clay works, which were then propelled to the sidings at Wenford Bridge by the following day's train.

Above: A little earlier that morning, the guard of the daily goods had dropped off a parcel at Hellandbridge before the train resumed its leisurely progress up the valley under the rapt gaze of some 'railway children'.

Above: At 3.25pm on 14 July 1962, 4-6-0 No 6921 *Borwick Hall* arrives at Penzance with what may have been the late-running 7.58am Plymouth parcels, due in at 1.5pm. In the background, along the shore of Mount's Bay, are Ponsandane sidings, Long Rock engine shed and Marazion.

Right: Earlier that afternoon, Laira 4-6-0 No 7916 *Mobberley Hall* runs into St Erth shortly after 1.35pm with the 1.20pm Penzance to Truro 'all stations'. On the down line can be seen the rear vehicle of the 11.50pm (Friday) Liverpool to Penzance service hauled by 'Warship' class diesel-hydraulic No D861 *Vigilant*.

Above: With its destination already in sight, the 10-coach St Ives portion of the down summer Saturday 'Cornish Riviera Express' snakes its way around the seashore cliffs to Carbis Bay, behind double-headed 2-6-2Ts Nos 4549 and 4566 on 19 August 1961.

Right: Although most people saw the St Ives branch only during the summer months, it maintained a lively service throughout the year. With daffodils spelling out 'Carbis Bay', 2-6-2T No 4566 arrives with the 4.32pm from St Ives on 17 March 1960.

Left: On my visits, the Helston branch always seemed to be very busy, perhaps not so much with passengers, but certainly with goods traffic. That the passenger service had been withdrawn before the end of the year in which this picture was taken was regrettable, but that in only another two years the goods service had also gone, was surely verging on the criminal. On 3 March 1962 the station appears to be full of traffic, as Driver Holloway washes out his china tea cup before departing on 2-6-2T No 4570 with the 3.30pm from Helston to Gwinear Road.

Right: In the 19th century, Hayle had been a hive of industrial activity, including the mighty Hayle Foundry and the western terminus of the Hayle Railway. This line climbed from Hayle wharfside to Redruth, using inclined planes at Angarrack and Penponds. The subsequent West Cornwall Railway rebuilt this line at a higher level through Hayle, necessitating a steep connection down to the original wharfside.
   On 14 July 1961, the shunting of Hayle wharves completed, 0-6-0PT No 3635 stands on the swingbridge across the canal, contemplating the climb back up to the main line, once the level crossing gates across the main A30 road have been opened.

Left: I don't remember now what the joke was, but the crew of 2-6-2T No 5537 seem to be mightily amused at our arrival at St Agnes on Saturday 29 August 1959. They were evidently running late with the 2.58pm from Chacewater to Newquay, because the two trains should have crossed at Perranporth. The signalman is standing ready with the train staff for the next section to Chacewater. My train was the 2.55pm from Newquay, hauled by 2-6-2T No 5552.

Above: In this view St Agnes station is situated at the top left, and 0-6-0PT No 3709 has just left for Mount Hawke Halt and Chacewater with the 3.20pm from Newquay on 10 July 1961.

Above: At 3.0pm on a summer Saturday afternoon, most of Truro's larger engines would have been out on the main line and only the Falmouth and Newquay branch engines are coming on or going off shed. 2-6-2Ts Nos 4593, 5537 and 5515 stand at the station end of the shed yard on 2 July 1960.

Right: On their way down from Drinnick Mill to Burngullow on 13 July 1961, 0-6-0PTs Nos 9755 and 1624 stopped to shunt three empty wagons into New Carpella sidings before resuming their advisedly slow progress down to the main line.

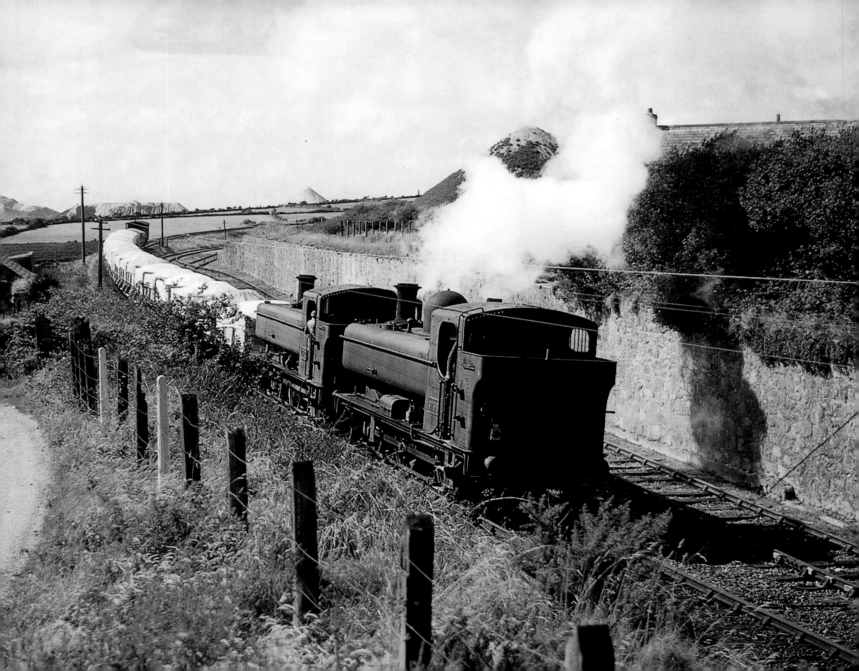

Above: Local trains are crossing at Luxulyan on the Par to Newquay line. The low stone station building, standing well back from the line, dates from Cornwall Mineral Railway days, but the island platform layout was installed by the GWR in 1910. In the foreground, the 12.25pm from Par to Newquay runs in behind 4-6-0 No 6812 *Chesford Grange*, while sister engine No 6875 *Hindford Grange* waits with the 11.52am from Newquay on 8 July 1961.

Right: 0-6-0PT No 1664 approaches Middleway Crossing, St Blazey, with the return working of the Goonbarrow branch goods on 13 July 1961. Alongside is the 'river of milk' or clay waste which then flowed into St Austell Bay.

Left: The Lostwithiel to Fowey line started life as a broad-gauge independent railway, only as far as Carne Point, following the western bank of the River Fowey. In this 3 April 1961 view, 0-4-2T No 1468 is hurrying out of Lostwithiel with the 2.25pm to Fowey.

Above: At the other end of the branch, Fowey station is looking very smart on 18 March 1961, with a 12/60 'paint date' on the awning. On the right, 0-6-0PT No 8719 is returning to St Blazey via Pinnock Tunnel, after shunting on the jetties, while auto-trailers W163W and W193W with 0-4-2T No 1468 form the 1.45pm to Lostwithiel.

Above: Although, even in summer, there were no trains on Sundays, when passengers were directed to the Southern National omnibus, the Bodmin Road to Wadebridge line had a quite intensive weekday service, augmented on Saturdays with through trains to and from Padstow, as well as short workings to Bodmin General. On one of the latter, the 12 noon from Bodmin Road, 2-6-2T No 4569 hauls a lightly loaded 'B' set on 10 September 1960.

Right: At the other end of the line, later the same day, No 4569 is returning with the 3.24pm from Wadebridge following the River Camel towards Grogley Halt, backed by Polgeel Wood.

Above: Nearing the end of regular steam working on the Looe branch, 2-6-2T No 4574 attacks the approaching 1-in-40 climb to Liskeard with the 12.15pm from Looe on 2 September 1961. Coombe Junction signalbox was then the centre of operations on the line, controlling the junction between the Looe and Liskeard lines, as well as the engines 'running around' their trains and access to and from the line up the valley to Moorswater engine shed and clay works.

Right: As 2-6-2T No 5557 leaves Sandplace for Looe on 18 April 1960, it enters a world of unfenced 'Continental' freedom with the 1.23pm from Liskeard. Watercourses on either side of the line seem to have made fences unnecessary.

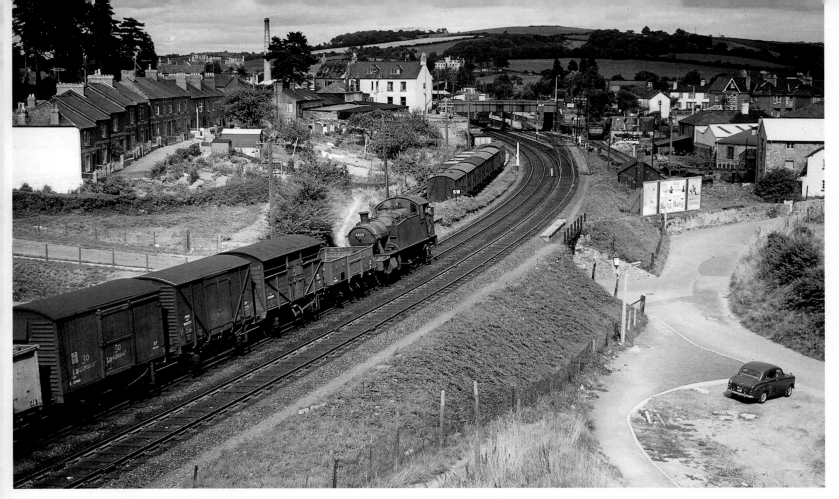

Left: Expectant seagulls gather round the fishermen gutting their catch below, as 0-6-0PT No 6410 takes a 'sandwich' auto onto the Royal Albert Bridge. This is the 4.40pm service from Saltash to Plymouth on 29 September 1959, composed of three ex-GWR and one BR-built trailers, Nos W163W, W229W, W167W and W189W. The Royal Albert Bridge was celebrating its centenary that year and was floodlit each evening for that summer only.

Above: At one time, Newton Abbot despatched three local goods trains daily to Totnes or beyond, one to Ivybridge, one to Kingsbridge and one to Ashburton. By 1961 the first two had been combined, and 2-6-2T No 5525 is bringing the return working into Totnes, bound for Hackney yard, Newton Abbot. Meanwhile, the Ashburton goods was now operating from Tavistock Junction yard outside Plymouth. Under the road bridge, 2-6-2T No 4561 is awaiting the road up Rattery Bank with the returning Ashburton goods on 18 August 1961.

Above: Only going down between Newton Abbot and Brent could the large Prairie tanks be used as pilot engines in front of the train engine. Any going beyond Brent had to be coupled 'inside', despite the delays this incurred. On the up road this formation was not, therefore, seen too often, but on 12 August 1961 4-6-0 No 4087 *Cardigan Castle* and 2-6-2T No 5164 are storming past Dainton Siding signalbox with a relief train to Wolverhampton.

Right: On the up through line at Newton Abbot, 4-6-0 No 5015 *Kingswear Castle* waits for the road with the 5.20pm Plymouth to Paddington return excursion on 27 January 1962. This was the first of four trains returning Tottenham Hotspur supporters to London after an FA Cup match with Plymouth Argyle.

Index of Locations Illustrated

Ashburton branch	30, 31	Luxulyan	68
Ashwater	54	Lyme Regis branch	15
Barnstaple Junction	47	Maddaford Moor Halt (near)	53
Brentor (near)	42, 43	Morchard Road	46
Budleigh Salterton (near)	17	Moretonhampstead branch	22, 23
Burlescombe (near)	4	Newton Abbot	20, 28, 79
Callington branch	40, 41	Okehampton	52
Coleford Junction	44, 45	Paignton	24, 25
Cowley Bridge Junction	12	Penzance	58
Dainton Bank	Front cover, 29, 78	Plymouth	36
Drinnick Mill branch	67	Plymstock	39
Exeter Central	13	Powderham	18
Exe Valley branch	9, 10	St Agnes	64, 65
Fowey branch	70, 71	St Blazey (near)	69
Goodrington Sands Halt (near)	27	St Erth	59
Halberton Halt	8	St Ives branch	60, 61
Hayle Wharves	63	St Kew Highway	55
Helston	62	Saltash (Royal Albert Bridge)	76
Hemyock	6, 7	Sidmouth Junction	16
Honiton Incline	14	Starcross	19
Ilfracombe branch	Back cover, 48, 49	Stoke Canon	11
Kingsbridge branch	33, 34	Tiverton Junction	5
Kingskerswell	26	Torrington	50, 51
Laira (near)	35	Totnes	32, 77
Launceston branch	1, 37, 38	Truro	66
Longdown	21	Wadebridge branch	72, 73
Looe branch	74, 75	Wenford Bridge branch	56, 57

Front cover: Day trippers are returning to Plymouth behind 4-6-0 No 1006 *County of Cornwall*, approaching Stoneycombe on the climb to Dainton Tunnel with the 5.40pm from Goodrington Sands Halt on 17 August 1962.

Back cover: Towards the end of a busy Saturday 'Battle of Britain' class 4-6-2 No 34079 *141 Squadron* and ex-GWR 2-6-0 No 6346 climb out of Ilfracombe past the Slade reservoirs with the 5.57pm to Taunton on 27 July 1963.